Craftsmen and Craftswomen

of the California Mission Frontier

Jack S. Williams
Thomas L. Davis

The Rosen Publishing Group's
PowerKids Press™
New York

To the early artisans of California and to Russell Ruiz Sr., Norman Neuerburg, Harry Downie, and Richard-Joseph E. Menn, men who dedicated their lives to the study and preservation of California's Spanish and Indian heritage

Published in 2004 by The Rosen Publishing Group, Inc.
29 East 21st Street, New York, NY 10010

First Edition

Editor: Joanne Randolph
Book Design: Corinne Jacob

Photo Credits: Cover, p. 24 © Francis G. Mayer/CORBIS; back cover courtesy of Jack Williams; p.4 © CORBIS; pp. 6, 37, 54 drawings by Father Ignacio Tirsch, courtesy of the National Library of the Czech Republic; p. 7 courtesy of the Bancroft Library, University of California, Berkeley; p. 9 © Archivo Iconografico, S.A./CORBIS; p. 12 courtesy of the de Saisset Museum, Santa Clara University, photo © Cristina Taccone; p. 14 Library of Congress Geography and Map Division; pp. 18, 22, 36, 39, 55 Dover Pictorial Archive Series; p. 19 courtesy Martin J. Morgado Collection, Siempre Adelante Publishing, Mission Carmel Museum; pp. 20, 32 © George Ancona; pp. 25, 33 courtesy of the Franciscan Friars of California and the friars at Mission San Luis Rey de Francia in Oceanside, CA, photos © Cristina Taccone; pp. 27, 45 (top) © Cristina Taccone; p. 29 collection of Mission San Francisco de Asis; p. 34 courtesy of La Purisima Mission State Historic Park, California, photo © Cristina Taccone; p. 38 courtesy Mission Nuestra Senora de la Soledad, photo © Cristina Taccone; p. 42 illustrated by Jack Williams; p. 43 © Hubert Stadler/CORBIS; pp. 45 (bottom), 46 courtesy Mission San Antonio, photos © Cristina Taccone; p. 47 courtesy Santa Barbara Mission Archive-Library; p. 49 courtesy Old Mission San Miguel Archangel, photo © Cristina Taccone; p. 50 courtesy Martin J. Morgado Collection, Siempre Adelante Publishing/Serra Cause; p. 52 photo © William B. Dewey; p. 57 original art reference by Jack Williams, recreation by Corinne Jacob.

Williams, Jack S.
Craftsmen and craftswomen of the California mission frontier/ Jack S. Williams and Thomas L. Davis.
    p. cm. — (People of the California missions)
Summary: Discusses why various artisans came to live and work in early California and describes the activities of some of them.
ISBN 0-8239-6280-6 (library binding)
1. Handicraft—California—History—Juvenile literature. 2. Artisans—California—History—Juvenile literature. 3. California—Social life and customs—Juvenile literature. [1. Handicraft—California—History. 2. Artisans. 3. California—History—To 1846. 4. California—Social life and customs.] I. Title.
TT24.C2 W55 2004
745.4'49794—dc21
                    2001007870

Contents

Craftsmen and Craftswomen on the California Frontier

There are few places in the world that are as rich in natural resources as California. When the Native Americans first arrived in California thousands of years ago, they began to collect food and build homes using tools that they created. Each group learned to use the things that they found in nature.

California is a land with many different environments. In the southeast there are hot, sandy deserts where rocks are more plentiful than trees. In the north there are high mountains and valleys with thundering rivers and lands covered by forests of redwood and pine trees. In the vast interior valleys there are seas of grass that seem to stretch into the most distant horizons. For the native peoples, there was an abundant supply of animals and plants. California was a land of plenty.

Many different groups of Native Americans lived in California. The first European visitors were confused by all the distinct languages that they heard. The Quechan, the Serrano, the Chemehuevi, the Yokuts, the Mojaves, the Kumeyaay, the Cahuilla, the Tongva, the Chumash, the Salinans, the Esselen, the Ohlone, the Wintun, the Wappo, and the Miwok called out proud greetings, which echoed over the hills and valleys. The Indians used an amazing array of survival skills. For example, they were experts at using plants as medicines. They harvested thousands of types of wild foods, including plants,

◄ *California has many redwood, pine, and oak forests. Giant redwoods like these provided an important source of lumber, which was turned into furniture, roof beams, and even coffins. These items were used throughout Spanish California.*

This Ignacio Tirsch painting shows two Baja California Indians preparing a skinned deer for roasting. In earlier days, the Indians hunted with arrows that had stone points. After the Spanish colonists arrived and trade was established, the Indians hunted with arrowheads made from metal and glass.

animals, and insects. There were many differences between the native groups, but there were also some common beliefs, tools, and ways of doing things.

Christopher Columbus arrived in the Americas in 1492. During the 100 years that followed, a new group of settlers reached the shores of California. These people came from the Spanish Empire, one of the largest and most powerful nations on Earth. The foreigners brought many new kinds of technology to the region. Technology refers to the way people do things using tools. The Europeans had a very different attitude about doing things with tools than did the Indians. The newcomers wanted to change the landscape that they found into one that would be more useful to them. To do so, they brought powerful new tools and building methods to California. Many Europeans believed that it was their right to use the land and its resources for their own benefit. This was very different from the Native Americans' beliefs. They believed that the land did not belong to anyone and that resources should be shared.

More than 200 years passed between the dates when the first Europeans landed in California and when the government of Spain finally sent colonists

The Spanish government needed craftspeople to build many different types of settlements on its new land. One type of settlement was a military outpost, or presidio. This is a painting of the Monterey Presidio, by José Cardero around 1791–1792, during a major reconstruction effort.

to make the region a part of its empire. When they arrived in 1769, the newcomers began to build several new kinds of settlements. They decided that they would have to create missions. A mission was a kind of town in which the Spanish government stationed representatives who worked with Native Americans. It was very important that the government establish friendships with some of the Indians. Unfriendly Indians could have easily killed all the settlers, had the settlers not had native allies. Without native help, the newcomers would not have been able to get enough food. During the early years, the missions served as a place where the settlers and Native Americans could exchange goods and ideas. The Spanish government believed that if the colony was ever to become a safe place to live, then some of the Native Americans would need to adopt the Spanish way of life. At the missions, the newcomers taught the Indians about the Roman Catholic religion and many new ways of thinking and doing things. The people at the missions introduced European styles of work and technology, such as farming and cattle raising, to the Native Americans. Franciscan priests were placed in charge of the settlements. Between 1769 and 1835, the Indians and newcomers worked together to create one of the most successful mission frontiers in all of the Americas.

Spanish government officials also decided to build towns, which they called pueblos, for Spanish settlers. The founders of Spanish California hoped that the towns would eventually grow into large cities, like Madrid, London, and Mexico City. Because there were dangers on the frontier, King Carlos III ordered his soldiers to build military settlements, called presidios. Like the pueblos, the presidios had many civilian, as well as military, inhabitants.

The newcomers brought many new technologies to California to help them create their new settlements. They used hundreds of different kinds of tools and machines. At first most of these items had to be sent to California from Spain or Mexico. As the colony grew, the settlers made more and more of the items. The secret to producing such advanced

This is a portrait of Carlos III, king of Spain. It was painted by Andres de la Calleja, sometime during the late eighteenth century. Carlos III, also called Charles, was king of Spain from 1759 to 1788.

technology was that some people worked at making the same things all day long. Over time the knowledge that such workers gained about these items allowed them to make improvements. Researchers call such people full-time craft specialists. They did not produce food or work at any other kinds of jobs. They became very skillful and efficient in their craft. Most of California's Native American groups did not have this kind of specialization.

The Europeans depended on specialists in various technologies to transform the things they found in the natural environment into useful possessions. These people are called craftsmen and craftswomen, and sometimes they are called artisans or craftspeople. No group of newcomers did more to change the face of California than did the artisans. There were many different kinds of craftspeople in early California. Some of the specialists worked in iron. Others worked in wood. Some artisans cut stones for buildings. Some craftspeople specialized in making shoes.

The craftsmen and craftswomen sent to California played an important role in the development of presidios, pueblos, and missions. As the Franciscan settlements grew and became prosperous, the missionaries decided to introduce many special skills that required expert teachers. Craftsmen and craftswomen from the nearby military settlements were hired to work as the Indians' instructors. Over time, more native people became experts and trained other Indians.

Learning from Experimental Archaeology

Information about California's early artisans is often hard to find. We do not have any way to go back in time and see the past for ourselves. People who want to understand these early artisans must study the available evidence. This kind of research often involves detective work. Historians study written records to understand the past. In some cases, they can use old documents to learn some of the craftspeople's names, information about the tools they used, and how much money they were paid. Unfortunately most of the details about the artisans' lives and work were not written down.

Cultural anthropologists study living people to learn more about how things were done. We can gain some knowledge about the lives of early artisans by visiting the inhabitants of the remote parts of Latin America. Sometimes these artisans still create the kinds of crafts that were manufactured in early California. Occasionally they use the same tools and methods that existed more than two centuries ago.

Archaeologists gain other insights by studying the traces left behind by the artisans' work. For example, the work done by early blacksmiths produced certain kinds of burned rocks and charcoal. These traces often survive long after the buildings and the blacksmiths are gone.

Some researchers create copies of old tools and other artifacts and then try to use them. These researchers come from many different fields and include archaeologists and specialists in living history. The people who work in the field of living history try to recreate as much of the clothing, houses, crafts, and tools as they can. Visitors to historic sites often find living history specialists who put on shows so that the public can gain a better understanding of the past.

Some archaeologists also conduct this kind of research. They often use modern laboratory equipment, as well as replicas of old tools, to determine how tools worked. For example, archaeologists cut up an animal, such as a deer or cow, then use precise measuring devices to determine how much the knife is worn. Based on this information they can estimate how long it would take for a metal knife to wear out. The researchers can use this data to determine how often a settler would need to buy or make a new knife.

Both kinds of research are part of the new and exciting field of experimental archaeology. Sometimes the investigators make mistakes. Creating an exact replica can be very difficult work. If a researcher makes something stronger or weaker than the original, he or she will probably not be able to determine accurately how long it will take to wear out. Other conditions in the laboratory may also influence the results. The effects of rain can make certain kinds of metal weaker. If a researcher does not take this into account, he or she might estimate that an iron nail or screw would last a lot longer than it actually would. Despite such problems, the new field of experimental archaeology has already produced a better understanding of the past.

Researchers conducting experimental archaeology often recreate native buildings, like this Ohlone house from the de Saisset Museum of Santa Clara University. The archaeologists use the same tools and construction materials used by the early Native Americans in order to learn more about how these people built and used the structures.

◄ 13

Who Were the Artisans?

The craftsmen and craftswomen of early California came from many different places. Like most of the other colonists who came to the region, they represented a mixture of people of European, Native American, African, and Asian heritage. Most of the artisans were not born in Spain, but in some other part of the Spanish Empire. Spain's empire stretched around the world. Spanish colonies could be found in South America, North America, Asia, North Africa, and Europe. Some of the Californian artisans were the children, grandchildren, and great-grandchildren of earlier colonists. There were also some craftspeople whose ancestors came from lands that Spain had conquered.

The Europeans who moved to colonial Mexico married people of many different races. They included those whom we would now call Native Americans, Blacks, and Asians. Although they had many different racial histories, the settlers who came to colonial California had a common language and a similar set of beliefs. They were all members of the Spanish Empire and the Roman Catholic Church, and they all spoke Spanish.

Wherever their families had come from, the artisans nearly all considered themselves to be Spanish. Compared to the other kinds of frontier settlers,

This map of Europe was created by Frederico de Wit around 1700. At this time, Spain, outlined in blue, owned many parts of the world. Some of the lands in
◄ *the Spanish Empire included the islands in the western Mediterranean as well as Sicily, in green. They also owned southern Italy (all of Italy is outlined in yellow) and a large part of North Africa, outlined in pink.*

such as mission Indians, these newcomers were less likely to preserve family traditions that had originated outside of Europe. Nearly every artisan dreamt of improving his or her life through his or her skills. By choosing to live as artisans, these people were deeply committed to finding a place for themselves and their families within the Spanish tradition.

Learning a Trade

How did a person become an artisan? Most of the craftspeople who came to early California had spent many years learning their trades. Spanish laws allowed male artisans to form special groups called guilds, or *gremios*. These organizations set up all sorts of rules about how a person could do a particular job. If a member's goods did not meet a guild's standards, its judges could throw him out of the guild and destroy all of his products. The members kept secret many of the methods that they used to complete their work. They also voted on who could join the guild.

Many of the members were the sons of families who had worked at the same trade for several generations. Other people became artisans by joining a master craftsman, or maestro, as an apprentice. The early Californians called these people *aprendices*. An apprentice is a kind of specialist-in-training.

Sometimes poor parents would try to improve their sons' lives by getting them into a trade. When a boy was about fourteen years old, his father would seek out senior craftsmen. In exchange for a fee, the artisan would agree to train the youth. The young man would move into the house or workshop of his master. During the years that followed, the young man would work as a servant and an assistant to his master. His training included instruction in reading, writing, and arithmetic, all skills that are important to

operating a business. An apprentice had to learn all the different jobs that his master did.

An apprentice was eligible to graduate to the status of a journeyman, or *mancebo*, after five to eight years. The journeymen did all the same kinds of work as the masters, but they received less pay and had fewer privileges. After another two to four years, a journeyman could apply for regular membership in a guild. In order to gain admission and be recognized as a master craftsman, the journeyman had to demonstrate his skills and pay a special fee. The members would ask him to prepare an example of his best work. The journeyman would use the item to showcase all of his abilities as a craftsman. The members of the guild would judge

Cedar crates that were shipped from Mexico City as packaging were used to build this confessional. It is mentioned in the inventory of Mission Carmel in 1779.

A blacksmith shows his apprentices the skills of the craft. Many of California's smiths were trained in colonial Mexico in factories similar to the one shown in this engraving from Denis Diderot's colonial-era encyclopedia. It could take up to 12 years for an apprentice to be considered a master craftsman.

the quality of his work. If the majority approved, the work would be declared a masterpiece. The guild would then publicly announce that the journeyman was a master craftsman. He would finally be able to leave the home of his teacher and open his own shop.

Although women were not allowed to join guilds, some women still developed reputations as skilled artisans working in important trades such as embroidering, tailoring, or weaving. These demanding skills were essential to the frontier communities.

The guilds did not allow women to join. However, on the frontier most craftsmen ran their shops as family businesses. Many of the wives and daughters of male artisans learned skills from their husbands and fathers. Everyone in the family usually worked together to complete the projects. The artisan families also tried to marry their daughters to other artisan families, or to artisans' apprentices or journeymen. By keeping the trade within their families, the craftsmen avoided paying outsiders, and they were able to grow rich.

Women artisans were especially important to early California. Apprentices and journeymen could not always be found. Craftsmen often had to rely on their wives and daughters to get their work done. Women were particularly important to the sewing, weaving, and spinning trades. Similar opportunities existed for women in other parts of Spanish America. Although they rarely received much credit, women's skills were just as important to the colonies' survival as were those of their husbands, fathers, and brothers.

By the time California became a Spanish colony in 1769, the guild system was falling apart. Many of the trades were then open to anyone who could learn how to do the job. Informal teaching arrangements were common. If someone living in a pueblo or presidio wanted to, he could offer to work as an assistant to a blacksmith or a carpenter. Many of the soldiers and farmers picked up important skills through this kind of arrangement.

The Artisans Come to California

In most of the Spanish Empire, craftspeople moved to places where they could find work. However, this did not happen in early California. From the start the missionaries and the army officers knew that they needed the special skills of these people. However, there were very few people living in California, and an artisan could not make a living working for so small a number of colonists. The government understood the need for artisans and decided to hire them and send them to the remote region. The first craftspeople in the province were government employees. Over time more Californians learned the artisans' skills and set up their own businesses. By 1835, California no longer needed additional artisans to meet their most basic needs. There were enough settlers and marketplaces to make it possible for a craftsperson to earn a living.

The First Artisans: 1769-1790

The military officers and government officials who planned the creation of California realized that the region would be so far away from any other settlements that it would need at least two kinds of special craftsmen to survive. They determined that to be self-sufficient and meet basic needs, each military base would need to have a blacksmith and a carpenter. The

Inside colonial workshops, such as the one in this engraving from Denis Diderot's encyclopedia, the carpenters used different types of saws, chisels, and other tools to perfect their creations. After the finishing was added, the pieces were ready for delivery.

Blacksmiths heated iron in the forge before hammering it into useful items. Francisco José de Goya y Lucientes created this painting between 1815 and 1820.

missionaries, who faced similar challenges, often borrowed these specialists to satisfy their needs. Before 1790, no other kinds of craftspeople lived in California.

Artisans called blacksmiths, or *herreros*, made things out of iron or steel. Every blacksmith had a special workshop equipped with a forge. A forge is a special kind of oven. Iron or steel objects were placed in the forge to be heated. While the pieces of metal were still hot, they remained soft. The blacksmith could form them into useful items such as swords, nails, spurs, and knives. He beat the iron or steel into the shapes he desired using hammers and a large iron block called an anvil. The smith plunged the metal objects into a barrel of water to cool and harden them. Because there were no sources of raw iron in California, the mines of Spain produced almost all of the raw material used by the blacksmiths. As a result, raw materials were very expensive, and the blacksmiths worked hard not to waste anything. If a large iron or steel object

could not be fixed, the blacksmith would cut the item into pieces and reuse the fragments.

The blacksmiths produced many different kinds of tools, including axes, hatchets, and plows. They also created many types of building hardware, such as hinges, nails, and door locks. They spent a lot of time making repairs to metal objects. Most of the early smiths also worked on guns, which required even

This lock and key came from Mission San Luis Rey. They were probably made by a blacksmith during the Spanish colonial period.

more specialization. Each of the soldiers' and settlers' pistols and muskets was made by hand. None of them had interchangeable parts. If something broke, the blacksmith had to handcraft a replacement.

The frontier blacksmiths of California and the Southwest were famous for their skills. They made many pieces that still survive today. Sometimes they would decorate their work with beautiful decorations. They were as much artists as they were manufacturers.

Carpenters were also very important to the early settlements. These artisans made various wooden parts of buildings, as well as a number of other useful items. Their products included roof beams, doors, windows, coffins, various tools, and wooden planks used in roofs and floors. They also built furniture, such as chests, beds, tables, and chairs. Carpenters made many beautiful items that still survive today.

The carpenters went to the forests to get wood. Some of the trees found in California, such as pine, oak, and redwood, were ideal for woodworking. However, the carpenters had to be very careful about which trees they selected. Some of the wood that was easy to get and to work with rotted quickly. Sometimes the carpenters would have to haul logs for many miles (km). The carpenters often sent lumber in ships to southern California, because the arid region had so few usable trees. Every item was shaped using hand tools. There were no sawmills in Spanish California, so carpenters often used a variety of saws, hammers, and axes to cut their wood. They often put pieces together with wooden pegs or with strips made from animal hides, because metal was so scarce.

The carpenters played a particularly important part in creating the first European-style structures at the missions, presidios, and pueblos. Nearly all of these constructions were wooden buildings. The carpenters planned and supervised the projects. The rest of the population provided most of the labor. The carpenters continued to play an important part in the creation of more permanent structures, made from adobe, tile, brick, and stone. They erected scaffolding, a kind of wooden framework that allowed people to build high walls and roofs. They also carved planks, doors, windows, and roof beams.

The early carpenters had to be able to make replacement parts for many tools. They spent a great deal of time creating new handles for hoes, axes, and similar equipment. They also manufactured the wooden parts of

This reproduction of the carved entrance to Mission Santa Inés shows the kind of intricate artistry colonial carpenters could create. Since most of the settlements' buildings included parts made from wood, carpenters supervised many mission constructions. Carpenters have used the River of Life design on this door as a sign that one enters the church through the waters of baptism.

weapons, such as the handles of muskets and pistols. Working with the blacksmiths, they produced long spears. Later the carpenters worked closely with the leatherworkers to produce saddles, beds, and chairs.

The carpenters often decorated their work with paint or carvings. Unfortunately, because wood is not very durable, we have far fewer pieces of their work than we do the products of the blacksmiths and some of the other artisans. In New Mexico, there are carpenters who continue to produce colonial styles of furniture in the present era. Modern furniture makers throughout the United States have incorporated many Spanish colonial styles in their pieces.

Most of the first blacksmiths and carpenters were also soldiers who lived and worked at the presidios. The officers excused the military artisans from some of their regular army duties. They also paid these men small amounts of additional pay. During these early years, it seems that very few women worked alongside their husbands or fathers at these two trades. After 1790, some women probably worked at carpentry. However, the physical strength required for metalworking prevented them from finding employment as blacksmiths.

During the early years, the missions did not have their own blacksmiths, carpenters, or any other kinds of artisans. When a new settlement was founded, some soldiers were usually assigned to help construct the first buildings. The military artisans helped. Later on, when the missions grew larger, they often borrowed or hired the army blacksmiths and carpenters to work for them for short periods. By 1790, some of the Indians were being given lessons in these trades. Eventually, the older missions no longer needed outside help . Some of the Indian artisans were even hired to work at the presidios and pueblos.

The Coming of New Artisans: 1790–1834

By 1790, the growing population of California was experiencing many shortages. Governor Pedro Fages realized that the province needed tailors, shoemakers, architects, construction experts, tile makers, pottery makers, and specialists in dozens of other trades. At the missions the Franciscans also declared their need for similar specialists. Both army and church officials hoped that they could find teachers who could train the Indians and settlers in these

This eighteenth-century Mexican painting portrays King Carlos IV (left) and Pope Pius IV (right) bowing to the patron saint Joseph. This painting can be found at Mission Dolores in California and is typical of those sent to California to be used in churches.

trades. Even though the population of California had grown, artisans were still unwilling to set up shops in the remote province. Governor Fages and the Franciscans both begged King Carlos IV for help. In 1791, the government officials finally decided to hire additional artisans and send them to California.

The government had to pay each craftsman from one to three times the salary of a regular soldier. The amount was still quite small compared with what could be made in Spain. No one was paid according to the

amount of work they did or the number of things they produced. The exact amount they received depended on their qualifications and the size of their families. As part of their job the artisans were ordered by the king to teach their skills to California's settlers and mission Indians. Part of their salary was set aside to cover the costs of their students, who often lived at the craftsmen's homes as apprentices. The government also received a portion of the money paid for any items made by artisans.

After 1810, an increasing number of foreign artisans moved to California. These men included carpenters, painters, barrel makers, and millwrights. Millwrights were experts in designing and building various kinds of structures and machines that were used to grind grain into flour. However, most of the foreign artisans did not play an important part in the region until after the missions were closed around 1835.

For the most part the artisans lived with their families at the presidios and pueblos. Sometimes they were hired for short periods of time to work at the missions. Other craftsmen were loaned to ship captains or army commanders for temporary assignments. Most of the artisans' contracts were for specific jobs, such as building a new church. A few of the largest missions hired artisans to serve as teachers on a long-term basis. Once the artisans had taught the Indians their skills, the Native American craftspeople replaced the artisans as supervisors and instructors.

Manufacturers

Among the artisans sent to California were a number of specialists who manufactured things that the government hoped to sell. Throughout the Spanish Empire, there was a need for inexpensive goods. The king's officials hoped that California's craftsmen would eventually be able to sell their products to colonists living in other parts of Spanish America.

Many of California's officials believed that weavers could make a lot of money in California. By 1790, there were immense herds of sheep at the presidios, pueblos, and missions. Their meat was an important source of food. However, the average settler or mission Indian did not know very much about turning the sheep's coats into wool. Their limited efforts to hand-process the animals' hair only produced a few crude items, such as sacks.

The weavers taught the settlers and the Indians how to turn the raw wool into cloth. This was a complicated process requiring many different steps. First the wool was sheared from the sheep. Then the weavers and their assistants had to clean the wool carefully before they could spin it. Weavers used teasel cards to comb out the clumps and dirt from the sheep's cut hair. Wires or thistles covered the surfaces of these wooden devices. Once the wool was carded, it was made into yarn. In order to make yarn, the workers used a spinning wheel, or spindle whorl. The weavers were now ready to begin working at their looms,

The settlers brought many new types of tools and machinery with them to the new land. Among these was a large, wooden machine called a loom, which allowed the Indians to turn wool yarn into cloth. This replica of a loom can be found at Mission San Luis Rey.

which they used to turn the yarn into cloth. Weavers used a combination of hand and foot movements to control and power these large, wooden machines. It took many hours of careful work for a weaver to produce a finished product, such as a woven blanket, a sash, or a shawl.

Many settlers and Indians became skilled weavers. Unlike other trades that were introduced in early California, most of the people who learned the weavers' skills were women. The manufacture of cloth and clothing was normally seen as women's work. Nonetheless, women were not allowed to run the weaving shops. Although it was unfair, men were almost always placed in charge of the operations and took credit for the work, even when women often provided most of the expertise. The many skilled women weavers were treated as if they were nothing more than assistants.

◄ *Before a sheep's coat could be made into yarn, it had to be sheared from the sheep and then properly cleaned.*

 33

The frontier also needed people who knew how to turn the skins of cattle and deer into leather. Many of the settlers could create basic goods, such as bags and leather straps. However, few colonists knew how to produce the more complex kinds of goods that they needed, such as saddles. It was very expensive to ship these items from central Mexico or Spain. Leatherworking was hot, smelly, dirty work that required a lot of physical strength. Most of the people who worked in this trade were men.

Colonial leatherworkers created nearly all the saddles used in early California. The saddle tree, or frame, shown above was covered by layers of rawhide when it was placed on a horse. This example is a replica from Mission La Purísima.

The professional leatherworkers brought a number of important innovations to California. The settlers already knew how to treat chemically the skins of animals to make them into leather. This process is called tanning. The early settlers' techniques were crude and slow. The artisans known as tanners, or *curtidores*, taught the settlers and mission Indians how to use more modern technology to get this job done. They introduced large, cement-and-brick pools, called tanning vats, which could process many hides at once. The new technology made it cheaper and easier to make leather.

Horses were essential to the new colony because they provided the only means of transportation. Unfortunately, the cost of shipping saddles and other horse gear to the frontier was enormous. After 1790, the first saddle makers, called saddlers, arrived in the remote province. They manufactured all sorts of leather horse gear. They created saddles as well as all the required reins, girths, straps, and bridles. They also made a number of other kinds of essential frontier leather goods, such as the hide jackets and shields used by the presidio soldiers.

A cobbler, or shoemaker, was another kind of frontier artisan who worked with leather. Every cobbler had a vice that he used to hold the shoe in place while he sewed it together. The artisan held this tool in place with his knees. Every cobbler also had a set of numbered wooden molds that were shaped as feet. These molds allowed the craftsmen to fit shoes to a standard size. In some cases, customers would actually have custom molds made to match their feet. Either way, the shoes were not very comfortable at first. Instead of being made for right and left feet, both shoes that made up the pair had the same shape. They had to be broken in gradually. In addition to regular shoes, the cobblers also made leather leg coverings called *botas*. Riders used botas to protect their lower legs. The cobblers also manufactured several different kinds of sandals. In contrast with the saddle makers, all the members of the

*Another colonial craftsman was the shoemaker, or cobbler.
Here is a picture of a cobbler performing his craft.
Some of the tools that cobblers used included several
wooden molds of feet and a vice to hold the shoe in place.*

cobblers' families, including their wives and daughters, often helped them complete their work.

Artisans who specialized in rope making also came to California. The government introduced a plant known as hemp to several of the pueblos and missions. After the hemp had been harvested, a special set of wooden machines pounded and twisted the plants' stems. The artisans braided the long fibers into strong, water-resistant ropes. These ropes were extremely valuable to the Spanish navy. The ships that came to California from Mexico, South America, and the Philippines often needed repairs. The violent storms of the Pacific Ocean often damaged ships' sails and ropes. The Californians sold replacement ropes to the navy.

Tailors produced fancy garments like the ones shown here in this Ignacio Tirsch painting that dates from the middle of the eighteenth century. Fancy coaches, such as the one shown here, were never imported to California, though they were abundant in Mexico.

Craftspeople who made clothing also had to be imported. The women in the settlements knew how to make basic outfits. However, they rarely heard about the new styles that were popular in Europe or Mexico. A family that wanted to wear the latest fashions had to buy expensive suits and dresses that were made in Spanish America or Europe. The government officials agreed to send tailors to the remote province. These men, called *sastres*, specialized in making fashionable clothing. There were no sewing machines on the frontier, so every item had to be cut and sewn by hand. The wives and daughters of tailors usually helped their husbands and fathers to make the clothes.

sizes and shapes. The artisans and their apprentices could also make a lot more pottery in a shorter period of time using this technology. The vessels they made were attractive and also were less expensive than similar imported Mexican varieties.

The pottery pieces dried for many days before they were ready for baking. Sometimes the artisans would add a special coat of red clay to decorate the outer surfaces. The pottery was baked, or fired, in special ovens called kilns. If someone tried to use an unfired clay vessel, it would quickly crack or disintegrate. The work crews kept the kilns burning for several days. It took several more days for the ovens to cool. Finally, the artisans were ready to sell or use their pottery.

Each of the tradesmen wore a distinctive type of clothing and carried special tools that made him easy to recognize. Few craftspeople enjoyed the luxury of a separate building that could be used as a work area. Instead, most artisans combined their workshops with their homes. A few factories were found at the bigger missions. Here the large number of apprentices made backyard shops impractical.

Builders

By 1790, California was becoming a prosperous place. Some of the people living at the presidios and pueblos had begun to save money. Many of the older missions were also growing wealthy. There were plenty of workers and money to build better houses and other kinds of structures. The only problem was that the people who lived in the region did not know how to accomplish this goal. The government and the Franciscans asked the king to send artisans who specialized in building. King Carlos IV agreed to dispatch teams of these men from Mexico.

Even the most elaborate buildings created during colonial times were rarely erected under the supervision of what today is called a professional architect. Instead a craftsman called a master builder usually did this job. He was sort of a combination of an architect and a construction foreman.

The master builders supervised all aspects of construction. They generally came up with the plans and were responsible for including whatever features the sponsors wanted. Very few of these men drew their plans on paper. Instead they worked according to a design they kept in their heads. As the building grew, they made changes according to their ideas of how the finished building should look. Sometimes the master builders made mistakes, and the structures were either ugly or they collapsed. By the end of the colonial period, around

1821, architects had begun to replace master builders in major construction projects. Like modern architects, they went to school for many years to learn about mathematics and engineering, and they drew detailed drawings and plans of proposed structures.

One of the first jobs that the master builder had to do was supervise the manufacturing of adobe bricks. He had to identify sources of soil with clay, clean

Making adobe bricks takes many days and careful work. After they have dried in the sun, the bricks are stacked. They will later be used in building construction. This photograph is from a rural area of Argentina, where the colonial art of adobe-making has survived.

sand, and fresh water. The ingredients were combined in big holes called barrow pits. The builders used their feet to mix mud, sand, and straw. The resulting product was forced into rectangular wooden molds. The workers had to be very careful to get all the air out of the mud, so that the bricks would be strong. The sun dried the earthen blocks, or adobes, for several weeks. The crews turned the bricks so that they would dry thoroughly. Finally the workers stacked the adobes together in large piles.

The master builders also supervised the crews who burned seashells and limestone to produce quicklime. The construction teams used this mineral to

◄ *Simple houses of worship such as the one shown here were common in the early settlements of California. This painting based on a nineteenth-century engraving shows the chapel at the Presidio of Tuscon, Arizona.*

make plaster and concrete. During the first phase of the work, the Indians and settlers collected pieces of limestone or baskets of shells. They burned these substances in large ovens called kilns that were built into the sides of hills. It took about a week for the process to be completed. After the kilns had cooled down, the workers removed the chalky white powder and mixed it with water. After it had completely dried, the master builder was ready to use the new quicklime.

The artisans mixed the quicklime with a little sand, cactus juice, and goats' milk to make the plaster used on the inside of buildings. If sand was not added, the covering would often crack. The cactus juice and milk helped the plaster to stick to the walls and hold together. When they wanted to make plaster for the outside of a building, the workers used a lot more sand and did not use milk. The coverings used on the outsides of the buildings had to be a lot thicker than the coverings on the insides. The outsides of the buildings also had much larger surfaces than did the insides. As a result, builders could not easily get enough goat's milk to prepare the mixture. To make cement for concrete, the artisans added thousands of small rocks to the mixture. The master builders even had a formula for a special kind of cement that would harden under water.

A number of professional stonecutters came to the colony. Near Monterey Bay they recognized a kind of sandstone that could be cut easily using saws and special iron tools called chisels. Once the stone completely dried out, it became hard and would last for many years. The stonecutters used these kinds of blocks to build parts of the Presidio of Monterey and Mission Carmel. Portions of both

This wall at the Mission La Purísima has a tile roof. These replica tiles, or tejas, were made using the same techniques and wooden molds as those used by the mission Indians.

of these beautiful structures are still standing today.

Professional tile makers also played an important part in the creation of buildings in early California. Tile makers specialized in creating rounded roof tiles, called *tejas*, and flat paving bricks, called *ladrillos*. The ladrillos were sometimes used to create columns or to reinforce adobe buildings. The tile makers employed the same basic technology as did the potters. Instead of using pottery wheels, they made the tile with wooden molds similar to those found in adobe manufacturing. The tiles and bricks were fired in large kilns.

Millwrights were also very important to early California. They created facilities and machines that ground grain into flour. The mills made it a lot easier for the settlers and the Native Americans to make flour from wheat and corn. Without the

This close-up shows original roof tiles (top) and pipe tiles (bottom) from Mission San Antonio, in California.

This horizontal waterwheel was powered by water that shot out of the spout at the left. The water's force caused the wheel to turn, which powered a millstone in the room above. This waterwheel is a replica installed in the original mill at Mission San Antonio.

mills, the Californians would have had to do all the work by hand. The millwrights supervised all aspects of the mills' construction, including the cutting of the heavy grinding stones and the creation of the mechanisms that powered the facilities. Millwrights built several water-powered mills in the colony. The artisans had to calculate how much water was needed to move the heavy, wooden waterwheels that powered the machinery. The millwrights also created smaller, animal- and people-powered stone mills, called *tahona* mills.

Only a few of the people who came to early California had any skills as professional painters. Almost all of these professionals' work was done inside churches. One of the presidio officers became famous for his skill as a painter. His name was Lieutenant José de Zúñiga, and he painted the elaborate interior of the church at the Presidio of San Diego. A few of the fancy residences built at the missions and presidios also had simple painted

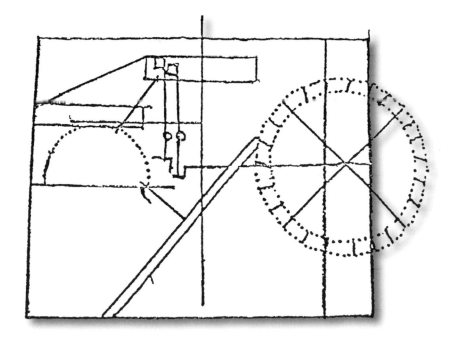

This 1820 drawing by Joseph Chapman shows a cutaway view of a water-powered mill used to process woolen cloth. The mill was built at mission Santa Inés. Many scholars believe it to be the first blueprint for a machine in California. The original sketch is preserved in the Santa Bárbara Mission archive.

decorations. Native American designs were also sometimes incorporated into the missions' decorations.

To paint the interior of a large building, such as a church, the artisans had to build scaffolding and use ladders. Large paper cutouts, called stencils, were used to lay out the designs. The artists and their assistants marked the patterns using charcoal. Some of the paints could be prepared using minerals that were found in California, but the artists had to import most of their supplies from Europe, Spanish America, or Asia. They sometimes mixed their paint with small amounts of plaster. This made the paint stick to the walls more easily.

 47

Home Life

The artisans lived like most of the rest of the settlers of early California. They occupied cramped, one- or two-room adobe houses. A family's furniture rarely included more than a low table, a couple of leather or wooden chests, a few wooden chairs, and a number of rough mats. The residents used the mats at night as beds. They did not have the types of fancy wooden beds that were found in the houses of wealthy colonists in Spanish and British America. The artisans' small houses usually served as their workshops, or *trapiches*.

Most of the artisan families cooked their food in small, private, open cooking areas next to their tiny homes. They equipped their kitchens with simple stoves and ovens. Food of all kinds was abundant in early California. The unmarried artisans usually arranged to eat with one of the families of settlers or the missionaries.

A few of the artisans had apprentices or other assistants. When they were not working in the shops, these people acted as servants. As part of their contracts, the government also agreed to provide many artisan families with one servant. All of these attendants helped out in the artisans' homes so that they could concentrate on their work as craftsmen. In the towns and presidios the servants, apprentices, and other assistants would have slept in their masters' yards or workshops. If no space was available they slept in the

This recreated stove at Mission San Miguel is similar to the ones that were used in larger kitchens and fancy homes in early California. Most stoves were built outdoors. ▶

open in the settlement's main plaza. At the missions, the Native American workers slept in the same housing as the rest of the native population.

Father Junípero Serra gave this small statue of Saint Anthony of Padua to Spanish soldier Francisco Ortega. It was used for many years in the Ortega family's home.

The artisans and their families were all members of the Roman Catholic Church. Every trade had its own special religious protector, or patron saint. The artisans were likely to show special devotion to these saints. They were always careful to celebrate their patron saint's annual holiday. The artisan families usually had altars in their homes where they kept small statues, or *bultos*, of these saints. Every day they would decorate the altars with flowers and candles. During the evenings they often prayed to the saints, asking them for help.

Most of the artisans who came to California had contracts that lasted for ten years. When these agreements came to an end, they had the right to return to Mexico. Some of the artisans decided to stay in California. They became the skilled artisans of the rancho period, along with the people whom they trained and their descendants.

Of course, not all the craftsmen and craftswomen ended their service by retiring or leaving California. The artisans suffered from the same kinds of illnesses and causes of death as did the other settlers who moved to California's mission frontier. Many of the trades exposed the workers to toxic chemicals, unsanitary conditions, or other dangerous situations. Construction workers were often seriously hurt in on-the-job accidents. Very few craftspeople lived to be more than fifty years old.

California's Artisan Heritage

Although there were only a small number of artisans in early California, they had a big influence on life in the region. Everywhere in California a visitor can find echoes of the Spanish architecture that the colonial craftsmen created. Spanish influences can also be found in furniture, clothing, and in many other objects. In many ways, what we think of as distinctively Californian can be traced to Spanish roots.

Nowhere are the craftsmen's and craftswomen's contributions more obvious than in the missions. Working with Indian people and Franciscans, artisans made remarkable progress in introducing complex European technologies. Few other Spanish frontier areas could boast the beautiful churches or manufacturing facilities that were seen in the largest missions. Nearly all the artisans that were sent to California succeeded in their goals of increasing the Indians' and the settlers' ability to produce the things that they needed or wanted. However, there was a price that had to be paid for these benefits.

It was the artisans who set California on the path of development that we can still see. Along with the settlers whom they accompanied, the craftspeople brought an end to the idea that the natural world was the one most suitable for people to live in. The colonial artisans believed that the

This early nineteenth-century painting of Christ carrying the cross was painted by Indian artisans at Mission San Fernando.

land, and all that it contained, was a source of raw materials that they had the right to change into their own designs. They felt that the world most suitable to humans was one created by humans.

At the beginning of the mission era, California's Indians were amazed and confused by what they saw. The strangers had so many things that could make life easier. For example, the cattle and horses that the Spaniards brought provided new kinds of food and transportation. The Europeans' steel knives and needles made sewing skins a far easier job. The adobe houses that the newcomers built could keep a person warm in the winter and cool in the summer. The foreigners had powerful technologies that made it possible for them to produce many types of new foods and even change the face of the land. At the same time, the invaders' lack of care for natural resources troubled many native peoples. It soon became

A European worker stitches a leather harness in this illustration by Denis Diderot. It was easier to sew skins with European-style steel needles than it was with the Indians' traditional bone needles.

obvious that some of the new technologies and habits had bad side effects. The cattle and horses ate many of the same wild plants that the Indians

In this painting, Ignacio Tirsch shows the decorative pattern of a piece of printed cloth. These kinds of designs were also painted on church walls.

depended on for food. The natives had to pay for steel knives and needles with long hours of difficult work. They discovered that the adobe houses were hard to keep clean, and were very dangerous during earthquakes.

Whether or not we agree with their ideas about building and creating things, we should remember the artisans of early California. They faced and overcame many difficult challenges. The craftspeople left an important mark on the world that surrounded them. They created many beautiful things that we can still see. The European colony, including all the missions, presidios, and pueblos, would not have survived without the artisans' contributions.

San Francisco Solano

San Rafael Arcángel

San José

Presidio
de San
Francisco

Santa Clara de Asís
Pueblo de San José

Santa Cruz
Pueblo de Branciforte
San Juan Bautista

Presidio de
San Carlos
de Monterey

San Carlos Borromeo
de Carmelo

Nuestra Señora de la Soledad

San Antonio de Padua

San Miguel Arcángel

San Luis Obispo de Tolosa

La Purísima Concepción

Santa Inés

Santa Bárbara

Presidio de Santa Bárbara

San Buenaventura

San Fernando
Rey de España

Pueblo de
Los Angeles

San Gabriel
Arcángel

San Juan
Capistrano

San Luis Rey
de Francia

Presidio de San Diego

San Diego
de Alcalá

Glossary

adobe (uh-DOH-bee) Brick made from dried mud and straw.

anvil (AN-vil) A large, iron object used in hammering iron and steel into various shapes. Most blacksmiths' shops included an anvil.

artifacts (AR-tih-fakts) Objects that show evidence of human activity.

artisans (AR-tih-zenz) A term for craftsmen or mechanics. People with a type of role that usually involves manual labor and the production or repair of material items.

barrow pits (BAR-oh PITS) Holes in the ground where clay was mixed with straw to make adobes.

blacksmiths (BLAK-smiths) People who make and repair iron objects.

botas (BOH-tas) A term used in early California for leather leg wrappings, or leggings. In modern Spanish this word means "boots."

bultos (BUL-tos) A religious statue. In colonial times they were usually made of wood, paint, cloth, and plaster.

cultural anthropologists (KUL-chuh-ruhl an-thruh-PAH-luh-jists) Scholars of anthropology who focus on the study of living peoples.

experimental archaeology (ek-sper-uh-MEN-tul ar-kee-AH-luh-jee) A field of study that uses replicas and scientific equipment to understand how things were done in the past.

forge (FORJ) A special kind of oven used by blacksmiths and other metal workers to heat metal.

girths (GURTHS) Bands or straps that circle animals' bodies to fasten things, such as saddles, to their backs.

guild (GIHLD) A kind of special society, also called a gremio, made up of a particular kind of artisan, such as saddle makers or goldsmiths.

jig (JIHG) A wooden mold that is used with a potter's wheel to make bowls and plates with uniform sizes and shapes.

journeyman (JER-nee-man) A worker who has learned a trade from one person, but who works for another.

kilns (KILNZ) Ovens used to dry clay.

ladrillos (la-DREE-yohz) Flat bricks that often were used for paving.

master craftsman (MAS-tur KRAFS-mun) An established worker with special skills.

masterpiece (MAS-tur-pees) A special product, such as a piece of jewelry, created by a journeyman to demonstrate his abilities in order to be made a master craftsman.

millwrights (MIHL-ryts) Artisans who were experts in all aspects of building mills and machinery used to grind grain into flour.

Resources

There are many places where you can learn more about early artisans in California. The following lists provide information about some of the more important resources.

Books

Kuska, George and Barbara Linse. *Live Again Our Mission Past*. Lackspur, California: Arts Publications, 1998.

The California Missions. Sunset editors. Menlo Park, California: Sunset Publishing Company, 1979.

Museums

La Purísima Mission State Historic Park. (805) 733-3713 (www.lapurisimamission.org)

El Rancho de Las Golondrinas, New Mexico. (505) 471-2261 (www.golondrinas.org)

Web Sites

Due to the changing nature of Internet links, PowerKids Press has developed an online list of Web sites related to the subject of this book. This site is updated regularly. Please use this link to access the list:
www.powerkidslinks.com/pcm/craftsp/

Index

About the Authors

Dr. Jack Stephen Williams has worked as an archaeologist and a historian on various research projects in the United States, Mexico, South America, and Europe. Williams has a particular interest in the Native Americans and early colonization of the Southwest and California. He holds a doctoral degree in anthropology from the University of Arizona, and has written numerous books and articles. Williams lives in San Diego with his wife, Anita G. Cohen-Williams, and his daughter, Louise.

Thomas L. Davis, M.Div, M.A., was first introduced to the California missions in 1957 by his grandmother. He began to collect books, photos, and any other materials about the missions. Over the years he has assembled a first-class research library about the missions and Spanish North America, and is a respected authority in his field. After 10 years working in the music business, Davis studied for the Catholic priesthood and was ordained for service in Los Angeles, California. Ten years as a Roman Catholic priest saw Father Thom make another life change. He studied at U.C.L.A. and California State University, Northridge, where he received his M.A. in history. He is a founding member of the California Mission Studies Association and teaches California history and Latin American history at College of the Canyons, Santa Clarita, California. Davis lives in Palmdale, California, with his wife, Rebecca, and his son, Graham.